WHEN FEATHERS FALL™

5 SECRETS TO SURVIVING INFANT LOSS THAT WILL TRANSFORM YOUR PURPOSE, UNDERSTANDING AND LIFE

---

*Special **FREE** Bonus Gift for You*
To help you achieve more balance and stability surrounding infant loss, there are
FREE BONUS RESOURCES for you at:
www.FreeGiftFromEmily.com
- In-depth training and insight on how can proactively process deep emotions, stop blaming yourself and achieve peace to create a more meaningful life after infant loss.

EMILY HARRIS®

Copyright © 2022 Emily Harris International, Inc. ALL RIGHTS RESERVED. No part of this book or its associated ancillary materials may be reproduced or transmitted in any form or by any means, electronic or mechanical, including photocopying, recording, or by any informational storage or retrieval system without permission from the publisher. PUBLISHED BY: Emily Harris International, Inc., DISCLAIMER AND/OR LEGAL NOTICES While all attempts have been made to verify information provided in this book and its ancillary materials, neither the author or publisher assumes any responsibility for errors, inaccuracies or omissions and is not responsible for any financial loss by customer in any manner. Any slights of people or organizations are unintentional. If advice concerning legal, financial, accounting or related matters is needed, the services of a qualified professional should be sought. This book and its associated ancillary materials, including verbal and written training, is not intended for use as a source of legal, financial or accounting advice. You should be aware of the various laws governing business transactions or other business practices in your particular geographical location. EARNINGS & INCOME DISCLAIMER With respect to the reliability, accuracy, timeliness, usefulness, adequacy, completeness, and/or suitability of information provided in this book, Emily Harris, Emily Harris International, Inc., its partners, associates, affiliates, consultants, and/or presenters make no warranties, guarantees, representations, or claims of any kind. Readers' results will vary depending on a number of factors. Any and all claims or representations as to income earnings are not to be considered as average earnings. Testimonials are not representative. This book and all products and services are for educational and informational purposes only. Use caution and see the advice of qualified professionals. Check with your accountant, attorney or professional advisor before acting on this or any information. You agree that Emily Harris and/or Emily Harris International, Inc. is not responsible for the success or failure of your personal, business, health or financial decisions relating to any information presented by Emily Harris, Emily Harris International, Inc., or company products/services. Earnings potential is entirely dependent on the efforts, skills and application of the individual person. Any examples, stories, references, or case studies are for illustrative purposes only and should not be interpreted as testimonies and/or examples of what reader and/or consumers can generally expect from the information. No representation in any part of this information, materials and/or seminar training are guarantees or promises for actual performance. Any statements, strategies, concepts, techniques, exercises and ideas in the information, materials and/or seminar training offered are simply opinion or experience, and thus should not be misinterpreted as promises, typical results or guarantees (expressed or implied). The author and publisher (Emily Harris, Emily Harris International, Inc. (EHI) or any of EHI's representatives) shall in no way, under any circumstances, be held liable to any party (or third party) for any direct, indirect, punitive, special, incidental or other consequential damages arising directly or indirectly from any use of books, materials and or seminar trainings, which is provided "as is," and without warranties.

WHAT OTHERS ARE SAYING ABOUT EMILY HARRIS AND HER STRATEGIES

"Having experienced loss ourselves, seeing Emily rise up and talk about an extremely difficult situation has touched us. It was us who suggested the title for her book, based on our own experience with loss. As believers, sometimes God blesses us in some small way to remind us He is still there. In this case, in our lives, Jeanette and I sometimes find a feather that is unique in some way. **It's like a feather from heaven or maybe, an angel feather.** Just so we can remember that our heavenly Father loves and cares for us no matter what we are going through. Especially in trials where we need His strength. May God bless Emily and her work through this book and in the future as she continues to use her journey to help others."

Bruce & Jeanette Clark

"Emily's story has such an impact and I know will help so many others across the world with her grace and willingness to be vulnerable. Infant loss is a difficult subject, yet the way Emily shares her story puts the reader at ease and shows the path to acceptance and healing."

Michele Fisher
Business Marketing Strategist
MicheleMFisher.com

WHAT OTHERS ARE SAYING ABOUT EMILY HARRIS AND HER STRATEGIES

"Emily shares tips that not only help you through your loss, but she also shows you how to preserve the memory of your child. Though I've not experienced this loss, I still found some of her tips helpful since I've also had two children pre-mature and spend 157 days with them in the NICU. So many emotions surrounded that time and so many people asked me very personal questions during and that experience that I didn't always feel comfortable answering. My favorite take-away from her book was. 'Only chose to talk about your child with those who are worthy of your story.' It brings a sense of freedom to know we don't have to share with everyone just because they ask."

Katherine Norland
Actress, Author, Coach and Filmmaker

"I was greatly touched by Emily's story and her ability to provide hope and inspire others who might be experiencing a similar situation. Her mission to bring a positive light to such a difficulty is inspiring!"

Ukpong Nwankwo, MD, FACP
Author, The Last Weight Loss Program You Will Need
Amazon Best Seller

WHAT OTHERS ARE SAYING ABOUT EMILY HARRIS AND HER STRATEGIES

"Emily inspires me and has helped SO many people teaching them how to survive infant loss and continue on to live a meaningful and purpose filled life! She is so professional at what she does! I appreciate all the work she does to help so many people!"

Dave Williams
#1 Amazon Best Selling Author 'Confidence for Life, 23 Proven Strategies to Increase Your Confidence for Greater Success' & Owner –
www.davewilliamscoaching.com

MOTIVATE AND INSPIRE OTHERS!
"Share This Book"

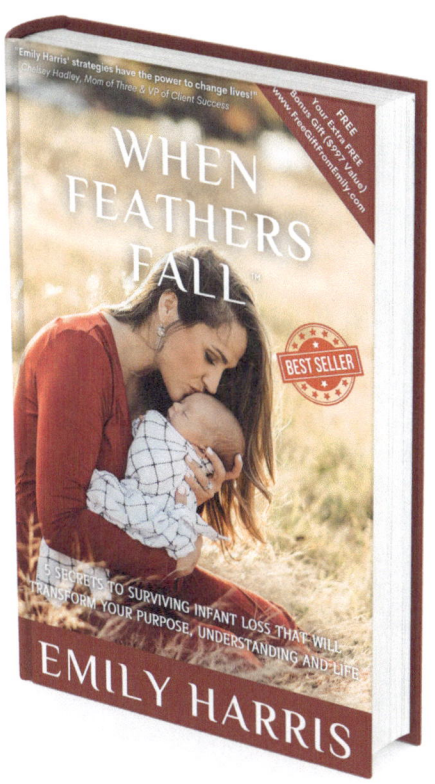

Retail $24.95

Special Quantity Discounts

5-20 Books	$21.95
21-99 Books	$18.95
100-499 Books	$15.95
500-999 Books	$10.95
1,000+ Books	$8.95

To Place an Order Contact:
Emily Harris International, Inc.
P: 818-797-4778
100EmilyHarris@gmail.com

THE IDEAL PROFESSIONAL SPEAKER FOR YOUR NEXT EVENT!

Any organization that wants to develop their people to become "extraordinary," needs to hire Emily for a keynote and/or workshop training!

TO CONTACT OR BOOK EMILY TO SPEAK:
Emily Harris International, Inc.
P: 818-797-4778
100EmilyHarris@gmail.com

The Ideal Consultant For You!

If you're ready to overcome challenges, have major breakthroughs and achieve higher levels, then you will love having Emily Harris as your mentor!

TO CONTACT EMILY HARRIS:
Emily Harris International, Inc.
P: 818-797-4778
100EmilyHarris@gmail.com

Dedication

It is with respect, admiration and sincere appreciation, that I dedicate this book to my wonderful family. Without you and the lessons you have taught me throughout my life, I would not have the blessing of being where I am today. Thank you from the bottom of my heart! I love you dearly!

Editor's Note

After the tragic loss of her infant firstborn son, Emily Harris' life was deeply changed - yet somehow she had not lost hope. This book is not about one woman's sorrow, rather, it is a moving meditation on the losses we all suffer and the grace that can transform us.

Many have published a lot of writings and devotions on grief and mourning over the years, but rarely, if ever, do you see someone who is allowing others in to glean in-depth insights into such a personal and sacred rhelm of their lives. That in itself is something to be cherished.

This book is a Christian classic for anyone who is grieving the death of a loved one or who has experienced great loss. We pray you are blessed and encouraged by the reading you experience today.

When Feathers Fall™

Table of Contents

Introduction: A Message to You!..27

My Story...29

Secret 1: Your Child Is Still Here..83

Secret 2: Celebrate Each Birthday...97

Secret 3: Create a Memory to Honor Your Child.........................113

Secret 4: Talk About Your Child...129

Secret 5: Know & Maintain the Sacredness of Your Child.........145

One Last Message!..183

About Emily Harris...191

Additional Resources & Mindset for Mom Course 193

Free Bonus Resources..195

Acknowledgements...197

A Message to You!

Being on this journey is something I never imagined, and certainly something I never would have chosen.

Finding meaning and purpose in the loss of my child has given me a new outlook on life and a connection with heaven I had never realized before.

In this book I hope you will find comfort, peace and most of all - I want you to know you are not alone if you're living a similar story.

Please feel free to reach out to me for support and as someone to relate to. Sometimes all you need is a little bit of hope.

I've been there, I've got you, I see you.

My Story

This story was originally published by Medical City Healthcare Take*Care* magazine. Spring 2019.

Scan the QR code to read the short-story magazine version of Emily's story:

https://medicalcityhealthcare.com/about/take-care/spring-2019

Joy and Heartbreak

"Emily's journey to motherhood was not easy, but Medical City specialists were with her every step of the way."

INSIDE

8
High-risk babies
Two years after his birth, Jacob leaves the hospital for the first time with a happy celebration attended by staff and well-wishers.

9
Three times the joy
The Sharps will always be grateful for the care they received at Medical City Lewisville during the birth of their triplets.

10
Best Place to Have a Baby in Collin County
Medical City Plano offers amazing care to expectant parents.

12
Cancer navigators
Navigators guide patients through all the stages of treating and living with cancer.

Wonderful care team
"The care team was so wonderful to us and made sure we lacked nothing. In that moment, we were at once complete." —Emily Harris

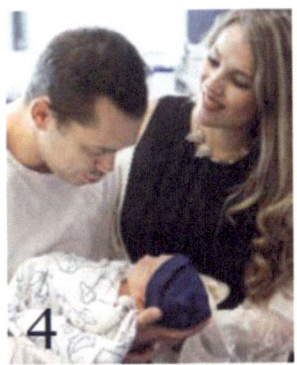

4

3-D MAMMOGRAMS
increase early detection of breast cancer by 54 percent and decrease callback rates by 37 percent. Call now to schedule your 3-D mammogram at **866-841-2335**. See page 15.

Next time you're online, look for us.

Health tips
Safety tips
Inspiring patient stories
Hospital updates

Also be sure to visit us at **MedicalCityHealthcare.com**.

TAKE CARE is published as a community service for the friends and patrons of Medical City Healthcare. Information in TAKE CARE comes from a wide range of medical experts. Models may be used in photos and illustrations. If you have any concerns or questions about specific content that may affect your health, please contact your healthcare provider.

Erol R. Akdamar	Kathleen	Janet St. James	Becky Frusher
FACHE	Beuthard	Asst. Vice	Content
President	Vice President,	President,	Specialist,
	Strategic	Strategic	Strategic
	Communications	Communications	Communications

2019 © Coffey Communications, Inc. All rights reserved.

Medical City Healthcare

Scan the QR code to read the short-story magazine version of Emily's story:

https://medicalcityhealthcare.com/about/take-care/spring-2019

Scan the QR code to read the full-length blog version of Emily's story:

https://medicalcityhealthcare.com/blog/entry/diary-of-a-first-time-mom-moving-from-loss-to-baby-joy

This blog was originally published by Medical City Healthcare on March 25, 2019.

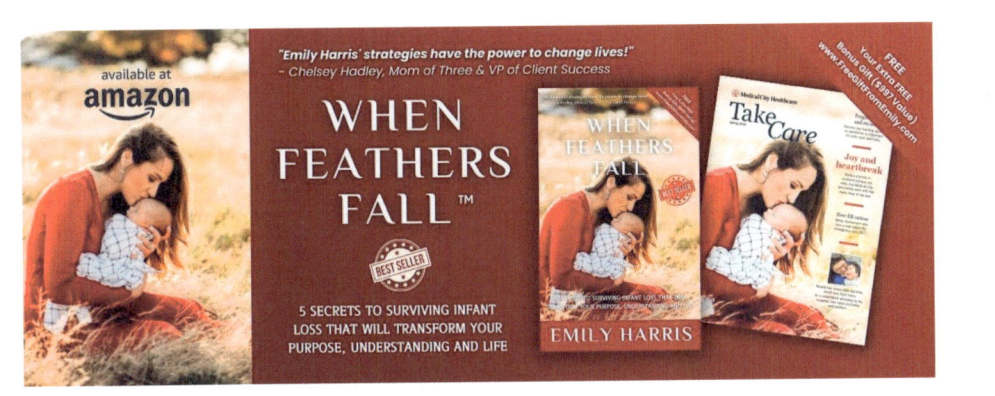

Scan the QR code for FREE resources and join the private community of mothers experiencing a similar situation:

https://www.facebook.com/groups/900950630756603

"Emily's journey to motherhood was not easy, but she has lived her life with grace and shows that there truly is power to overcome any obstacle. Her story is a telling lesson that it is possible to continue living your life with joy, satisfaction and purpose."

Diary of a First-Time Mom: Moving From Loss to Baby Joy

⌂ / Blog / We Deliver Dreams / Diary Of A First-Time Mom: Moving...

Medical City Healthcare - March 25, 2019

Share With Others

Meet new mom Emily Harris, a PR director in Frisco who gave birth to her precious son, Cason James, at Medical City Dallas. But not before Emily had suffered through endometriosis, looming fertility issues and the heartbreaking loss of her first son, Jackson Reed, from cervical incompetency when she was 20 weeks pregnant.

As a kid, I never thought about where I would be when I turned 30. I just thought about the then and now, and always knew everything had a way of working out. Study hard, work hard, do the right thing and the right things will happen for you, right? If my 30-year-old self could look back and tell that young girl something, it would be ... don't change a thing.

Find a Doctor

Meet new mom Emily Harris, a PR director in Frisco, Texas who gave birth to her precious son, Cason James, at Medical City Dallas. But not before Emily had suffered through endometriosis, looming fertility issues and the heartbreaking loss of her first son, Jackson Reed, from cervical incompetency when she was 20 weeks pregnant.

As a kid, I never thought about where I would be when I turned 30. I just thought about the then and now, and always knew everything had a way of working out. Study hard, work hard, do the right thing and the right things will happen for you, right?

If my 30-year-old self could look back and tell that young girl something, it would be...don't change a thing.

Being born in Harbor City, California, and having family roots across the state, racing dirt bikes was a way of life for many area residents. Everyone had dirt bikes and rode, that's just what you did for fun on the weekends.

Every chance I got, riding my dirt bike was the one thing I wanted to do since I first rode one at the age of 13. By the time I turned 15, I decided to try racing motocross. Some races went well and I brought home a trophy, others landed me in the emergency room.

I continued traveling across the United States with various racing circuits and entering all the categories that I could qualify for.

Never did I know that at one of the races I attended, I had just met the man I would one day marry...a born-and-bred Texan who lived in an up-and-coming town called Frisco.

Love and marriage...and a baby?

Fast forward to year 22 of my life, when Jeremy asked me to marry him. He talked about one day having a family, and I thought he was crazy.

Five years later, I decided to speak with my doctor about it, Monica Diaz, MD, an OB-GYN and fertility specialist at Medical City Dallas Women's Hospital. She was firm to let me know that if a family was in the future, it was a good time to begin planning for it — after all, I was now 27.

The thought was that it was going to take me a very long time to get pregnant, if I even could get pregnant naturally, as I had a large amount of scar tissue on my uterus due to endometriosis.

So in order to be deemed infertile, we had to try to conceive for one year (January 2017-December 2017).

After that year was up, the plan was to undergo surgery to remove the scar tissue and then evaluate if I could get pregnant naturally or if we would have to do in vitro fertilization (IVF).

Shockingly, at the end of February 2017, I found out I was about six weeks pregnant with Jackson.

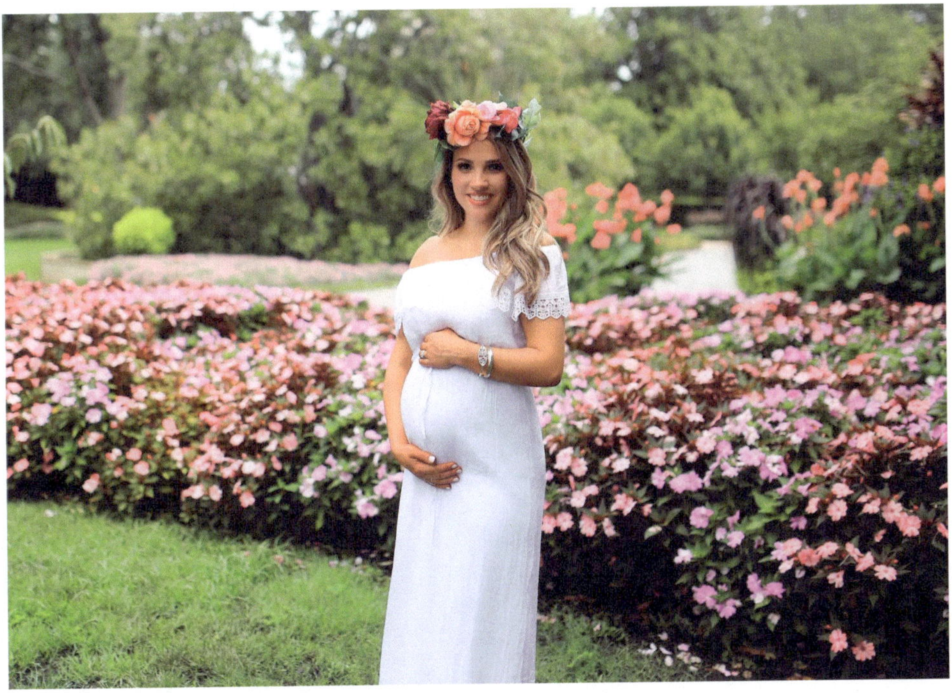

Baby surprise.

I was in shock and my husband was elated when Dr. Diaz confirmed that I was pregnant.

There were so many questions, but I knew we would find the answers and learn as we went. Upon recommendation, we decided to have prenatal testing completed with a maternal and fetal medicine specialist, Joshua Weiss, MD, also at Medical City Dallas Women's Hospital.

Each test we underwent came back negative for birth defects. The time had come, it was so real.

We picked out the most perfect crib to be the throne for this cherished child by one of us having the other select the item each of us liked. When we showed our selection to each other, it was the same one!

We laughed and picked the color of the baby's room, we joked about outlandish names and laughed until it hurt that this was our new reality.

We were parents. This was our son.

Baby bump.

Each day, the excitement grew along with my belly. Feeling Jackson move for the first time was a remarkable moment that one does not forget, and a 10-second video to prove it is all one needs to show every friend in the world that this is really happening.

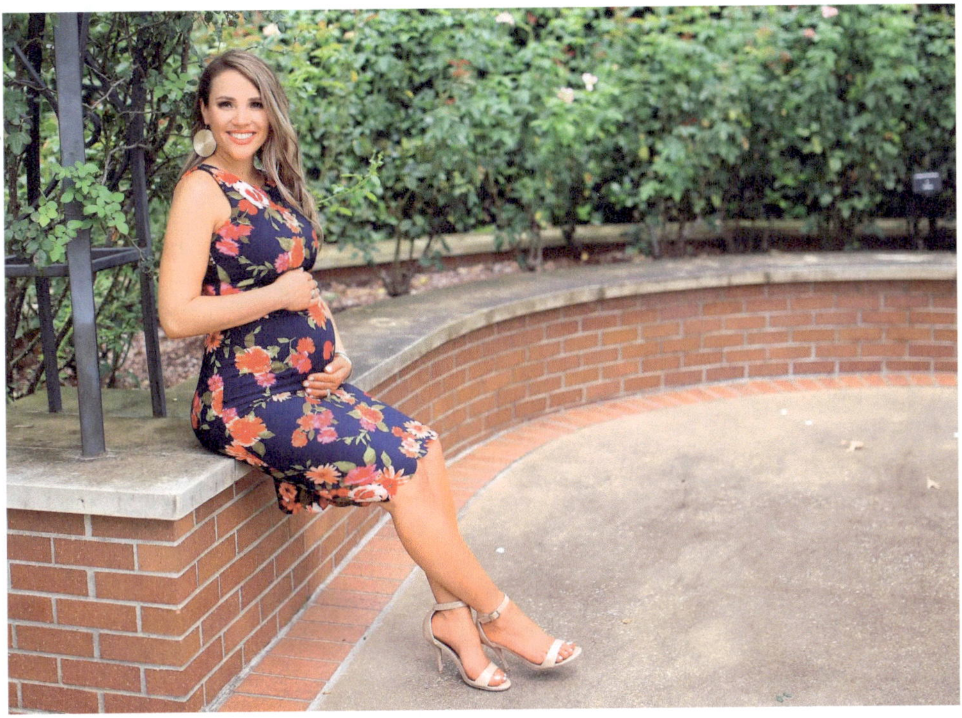

Going into my scheduled checkups was bliss because my son was doing so well. Carrying on each day with joy came naturally because in my mind at that point, a perfect future was set in stone — or so I thought.

It was Thursday, June 8, 2017. I was exactly five months pregnant when suddenly my water broke.

A late afternoon call to Dr. Diaz and a test to my amniotic fluid confirmed that the worst had indeed happened.

Right away, I was admitted in hopes that the amniotic fluid would regenerate itself and that my son would stay alive until he could be viable outside of the womb.

I was resigned to this, that there was hope and I would stay in the hospital as long as I needed to in order for this boy to survive.

Listening to his heartbeat had become a familiar sound and it seemed as if nothing could take it away. He's still alive, he's fine, I reasoned.

As my precious husband lay by my side in that hospital bed, the three of us were a family.

Everything was going to be okay, we told ourselves, this has happened to others and their babies survived, so our son would, too.

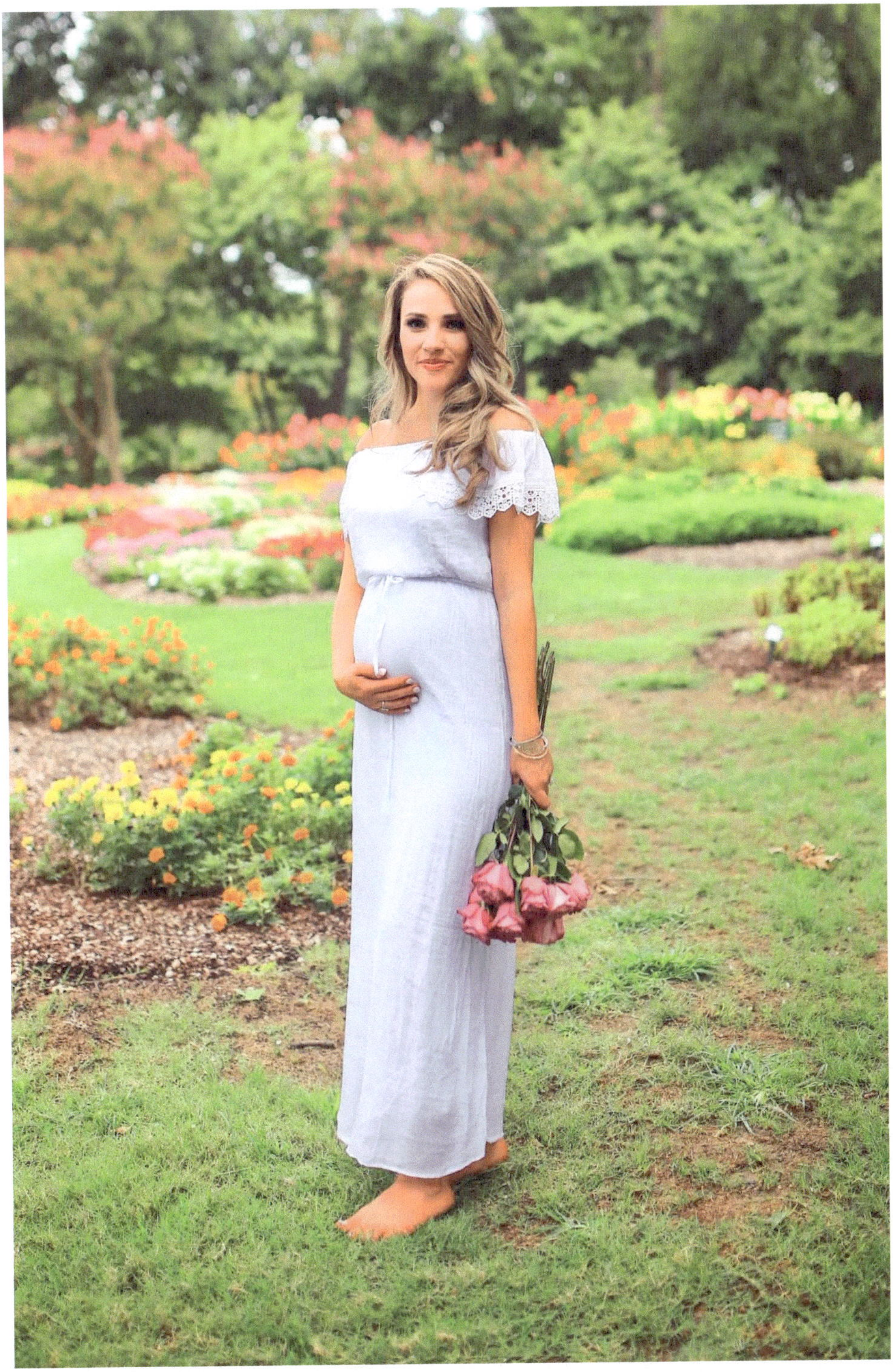

Sad goodbye.

At 7 a.m., our fetal specialist came in to make the final determination. He completed a sonogram and sadly confirmed that there was no amniotic fluid surrounding our child.

A test from the lab came back and brought Dr. Diaz to our room as she informed us that they weren't just worried about the baby now, but that I had an infection throughout my body from the amniotic fluid. "We have to save mom now," she said.

The most crushing words I had ever heard fell on my body, along with the weight of my husband. There were no words and not enough tears. We were transferred from that beautiful antepartum unit, that I suddenly so badly wanted to call home, into labor and delivery. The unit of joy, that to us, was full of sorrow.

The cries of newborns pierced our ears as we were taken to a quiet delivery room to meet our son. We listened to his heartbeat until it was no longer and sat in silent tears as we held him close.

This was our son, **Jackson Reed Harris,** and he was perfect.

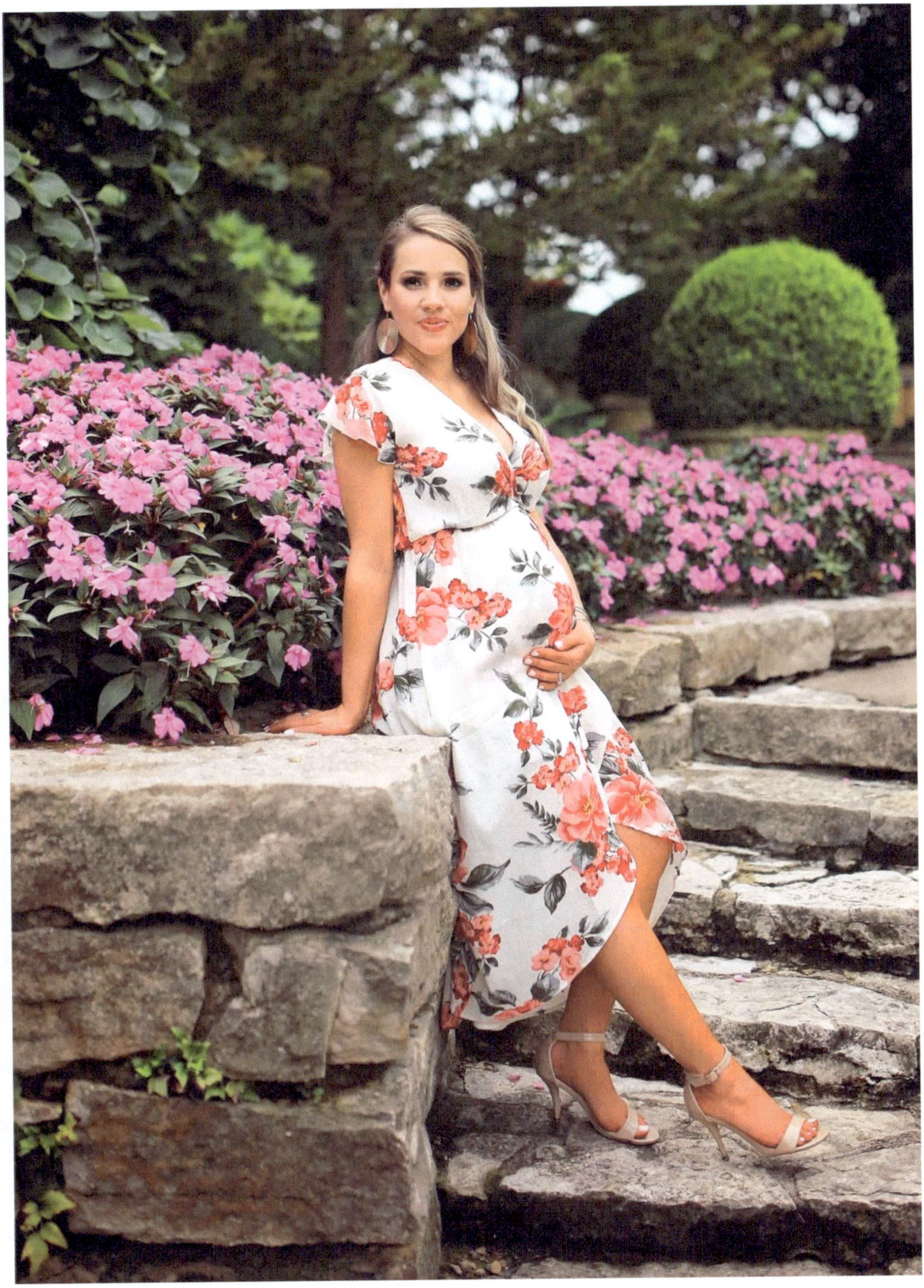

Bittersweet news.

Not knowing why my water broke early added urgency to a second pregnancy.

I had changed from naively thinking everything would be perfect, to feeling like my body had failed me and simply hoping we would have another chance.

Nine months later I found out I was five weeks pregnant. As exciting as it was, it was also bittersweet and overwhelming.

Would this child survive?

Without a word, my husband and I both knew we could not bear to bury a second child. We hoped desperately for a different outcome.

My checkups with Dr. Diaz went well. From the beginning, everything was normal just as before. In light of precaution beginning at four months pregnant, I was to receive weekly shots of 17-hydroxyprogesterone to prevent pre-term labor.

As the five-month mark drew near, I could only pray to make it past that day. What was a normal milestone to some was certainly a huge breakthrough to me.

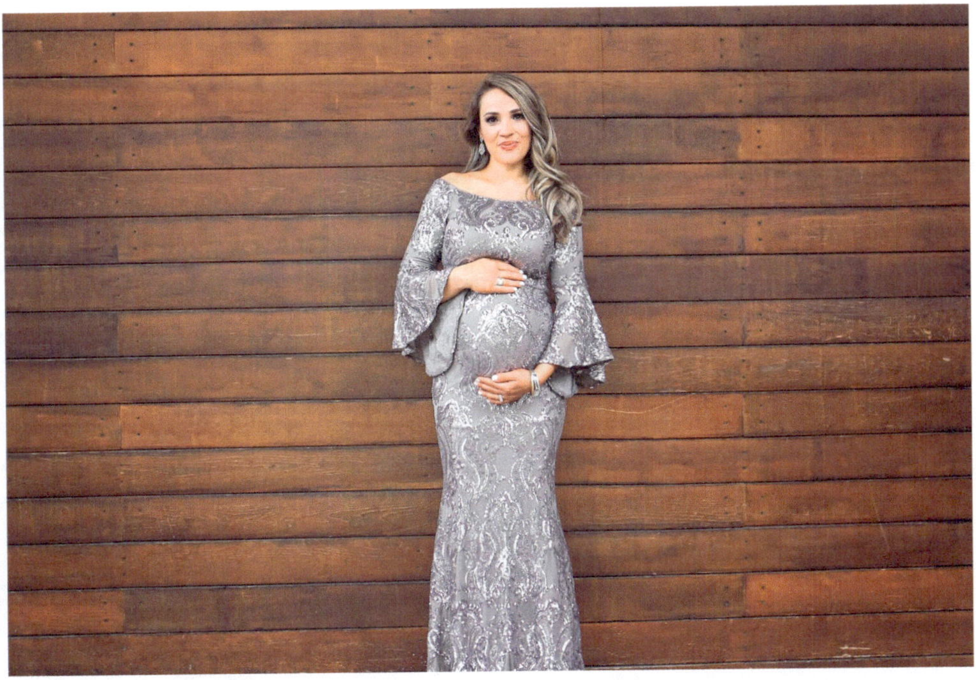

June 9...again.

June 9, 2018, marked a year since that terrible day... and I was now so grateful to have reached it again.

Yet just 12 days later, at 21 weeks and five days pregnant, I was admitted into labor and delivery again, this time diagnosed with cervical incompetency. The baby was trying to be born early.

Dr. Diaz explained that although there were risks of membrane rupture (aka, my water could break early again), Dr. Weiss would be performing surgery the next morning to place a cerclage (stitches) in my cervix in an effort to try to get my body to maintain this second pregnancy.

The excruciating loss of Jackson was imprinted on our minds as we pressed forward. If I did not undergo the surgery, losing this baby as well was an imminent reality.

The surgery went well, and we could only be thankful for any time that it bought us to give our child more time to grow.

The ten weeks between 22 weeks and 32 weeks went very well. I had been going to weekly checkups with Dr. Diaz to receive my hormone shots and to my weekly fetal checkups with Dr. Weiss.

At my 32-week checkup with Dr. Weiss, he determined that my cervix was shortening and the baby was getting ready for delivery. I was again quickly admitted into labor and delivery, this time to receive two rounds of steroid shots over two days to try to rapidly develop the baby's lungs.

We knew he could be born any day. From that point, I stayed on bedrest. We knew the baby would be born soon and any extra days we could get were small miracles.

We were at once complete.

At 37 weeks and four days, our second son, Cason James Harris, was born. This time, the tranquil delivery room was filled with excitement and expectation.

Knowing that we had made it this far in the pregnancy gave us full confidence that our child would be okay. Dr. Diaz let us know that our baby may have to be in the neonatal intensive care unit (NICU) for a short bit because the delivery was a couple of weeks shy of full-term, yet we knew in our hearts that the baby would be okay.

Many of the doctors and care team who were with us during Jackson's delivery filled our room to say hello. It was as if we received a big hug from our firstborn and knew he was with us in his own way. The care team was so wonderful to us and made sure we lacked nothing.

In that moment, we were at once complete.

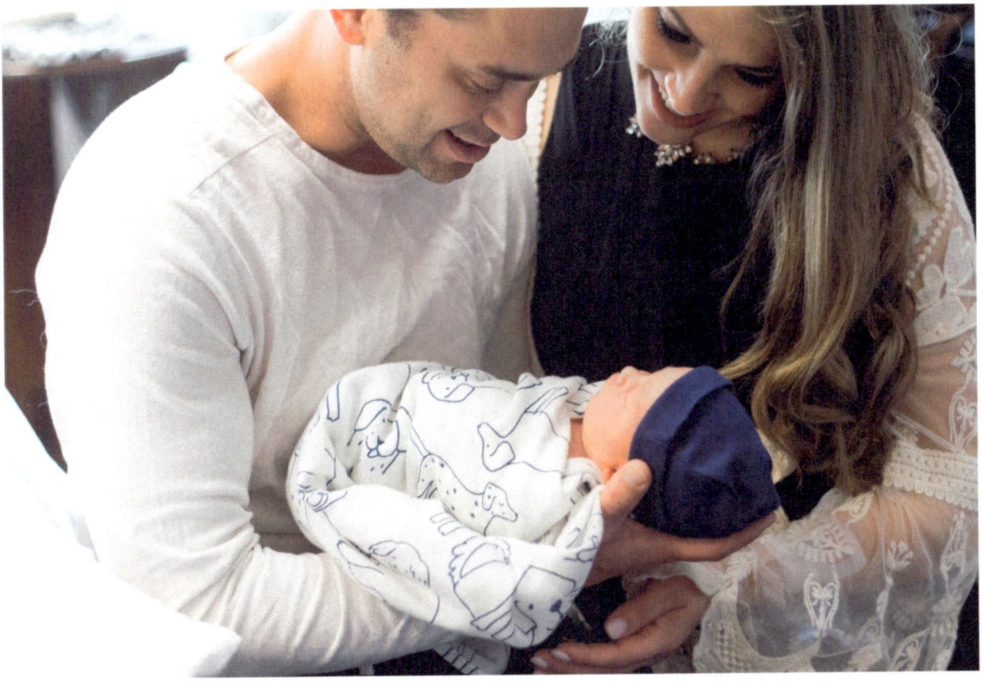

In heaven and on earth.

Looking back, I learned that the truly important things in life are people and that the ones who care for you the most are extra special.

It is people who are the gifts and are not replaceable.

Six months or a year ago, there was much uncertainty around my life, our lives, yet I knew we had to push forward in order to overcome the fear of the unknown.

Losing a child changes a person to the core, just as sure as gaining a child does.

I became a different person because of my experience. No longer did I feel that having a child could happen on my timeline, but rather I was immensely grateful for the opportunity I had been given to even become a mother.

As deeply as I missed that first son of mine, I was given a gift to love my second son twice as much. I have one son in heaven and one on earth, and now I can say with certainty that I finally understand life.

Cason James Harris was born October 18, 2018
Dallas, Texas

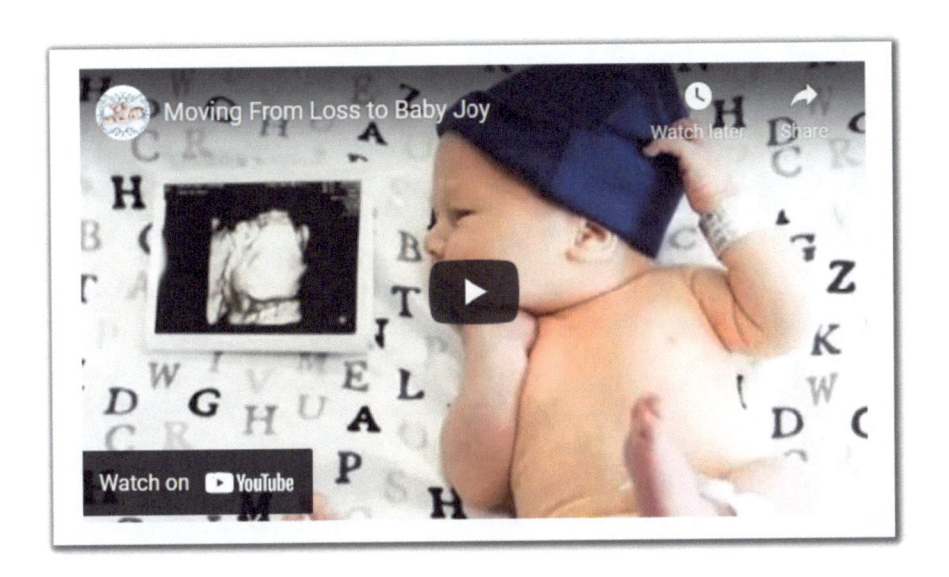

Scan the QR code to watch video on YouTube:

https://youtu.be/44rOjXrC8sk

About Emily

Emily is a PR director in North Texas and a first-time mom. She enjoys an active, outdoor lifestyle with her firefighter husband, Jeremy, and their new baby boy, Cason.

Medical City Healthcare women's specialists are experts at handling the medical needs of women no matter the situation, including high-quality gynecological care, family planning and infertility treatment, high-risk labor and delivery, breast cancer treatment, menopause management, osteoporosis solutions and more.

We don't just deliver babies. We deliver dreams. Find the perfect doctor for you or your baby or visit Medical City Virtual Care 24/7 from any computer or mobile device.

My goal with this book is to inspire and ignite you to do more and achieve more. Your child is proud of you and the world needs to know your story.

-EH

The greatest gift you can receive is knowing that you have made a positive difference in the lives of others.

My son gave me that gift!

I hope that my story breathes life into you to make a positive difference in this world, so that you can deliberately impact the lives of others in a meaningful and purposeful way.

-EH

Since I know you will want to ask, here's how I will know that you have made the appropriate adjustment on the first three chakras.

My senses are mentioned, but

I hope that my story has carried us into your life in the ways that give difference to the world, so that you can deliberately impact the lives of others in a meaningful and purposeful way.

SECRET ONE

Your Child Is Still Here

While the grief of your child's passing will always be near, what I mean by saying 'your child is still here' is, there are many ways that you have probably already noticed where your child will show up. It can be in simple initials that you may see on a sign as you are driving, it can be their very name imprinted on a keychain or at times a piece of clothing you may have worn when you were pregnant with your child.

Your child is still here, all around us, all around *you* for the rest of your life. Don't let others discount that and take the joy of the memories you have from you.

One of my favorite memories is when I met a little boy and asked him what his name was, and it was my son's name, too. It made me smile through my tears as I thanked the Lord for what felt to me as a gentle hello from my child in heaven.

Your child is still here, all around you.

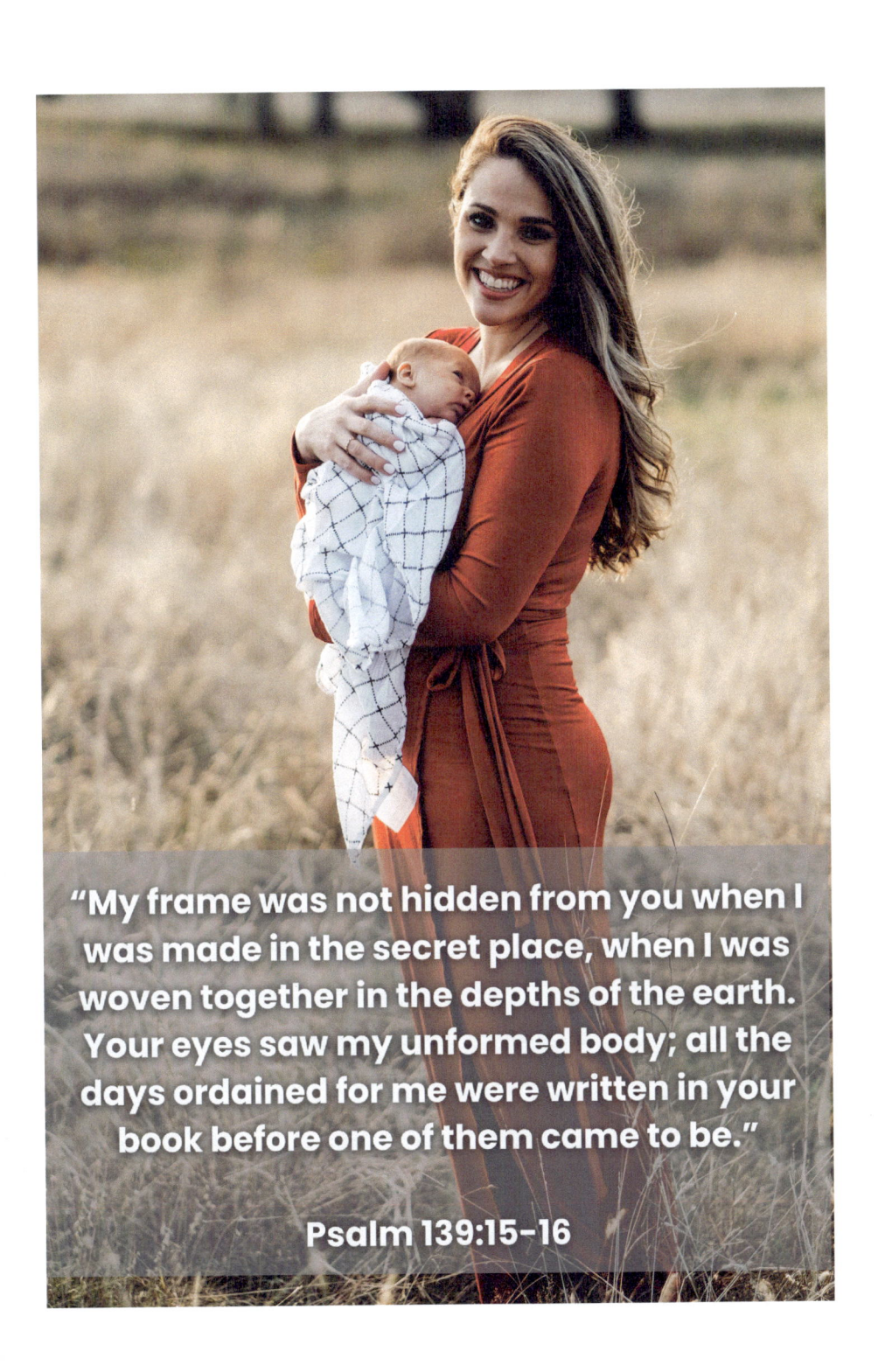

"My frame was not hidden from you when I was made in the secret place, when I was woven together in the depths of the earth. Your eyes saw my unformed body; all the days ordained for me were written in your book before one of them came to be."

Psalm 139:15-16

Secret One
Special Memory Session

Write down special memories and happy thoughts you have about your child.

_____
_____
_____
_____
_____
_____
_____
_____
_____
_____
_____
_____
_____
_____
_____
_____
_____
_____
_____
_____
_____
_____

"The heavens declare the Glory of God."

Psalms 19:1

Of all the things my eyes have seen, by far the best is you.

"I am He who will sustain you."

Isaiah 46:4

SECRET TWO

Celebrate Each Birthday

On the anniversary of our son's first birthday, our hearts were heavy - yet full. We had just found out not long before that I was pregnant with our second child. There was much joy, yet a freshly burned scar imprinted on our hearts from burying our firstborn son just one year prior.

We frequented the graveyard to visit our baby boy who had already changed our lives very much in that one year. So while we were extremely excited to have the opportunity to welcome a second child, we desperately hoped we would not have to lay claim to a second plot of earth next to our firstborn. As sad as it sounds, that thought was very real, and was our recognition of reality for the time being. We prayed fervently for a different outcome.

During the 12 months that comprised a year, I had become friends with one of the caregivers at the hospital who was our nurse when Jackson was born.

Celebrate Each Birthday (continued)

She thoughtfully created a gift box that enclosed the gender of our second child. My husband and I drove to Jackson's grave on his first birthday to spread roses and celebrate his life with a heartfelt balloon release. We thought it would also be very fitting to open the special gender reveal box quietly together in order to find out what the second baby's gender as a family. We opened it with our eyes welling up with tears because we could feel the weight and reality of this cherished moment. *It was a boy.*

To this day, opening our second son's gender reveal box at Jackson's grave is still one of my all-time favorite memories. He was there, he was with us and we felt his presence encompassed in our newfound joy.

Earlier in the week, we had hand written thought-filled notes to Jackson and sealed them inside the helium-filled balloons. It was our small but magical way of connecting with him in heaven. A large #1 balloon surrounded by clouds of blue and gold balloons were what we chose for his first birthday.

Through our tears, we timidly let the strings go and pensively gazed at the tranquil sky. Our hearts were immensely heavy, and overwhelmed with excitement and joy as we knew this second child was a gift from above.

So on June 9, 2018, one year after Jackson's passing, we began the annual tradition of celebrating our son's birthday with a very special and private family balloon release. It was just us and him, and we were grateful.

"The Lord gives, and the Lord takes away. Blessed be the name of the Lord."

Job 1:21

Secret Two
Special Memory Session

Write down special memories and happy thoughts you have about your child.

_____
_____
_____
_____
_____
_____
_____
_____
_____
_____
_____
_____
_____
_____
_____
_____
_____
_____
_____
_____
_____
_____
_____
_____

"Taste and see that the Lord is good."

Psalms 34:8

"All your children will be taught by the Lord, and great will be their peace."

Isaiah 54:13

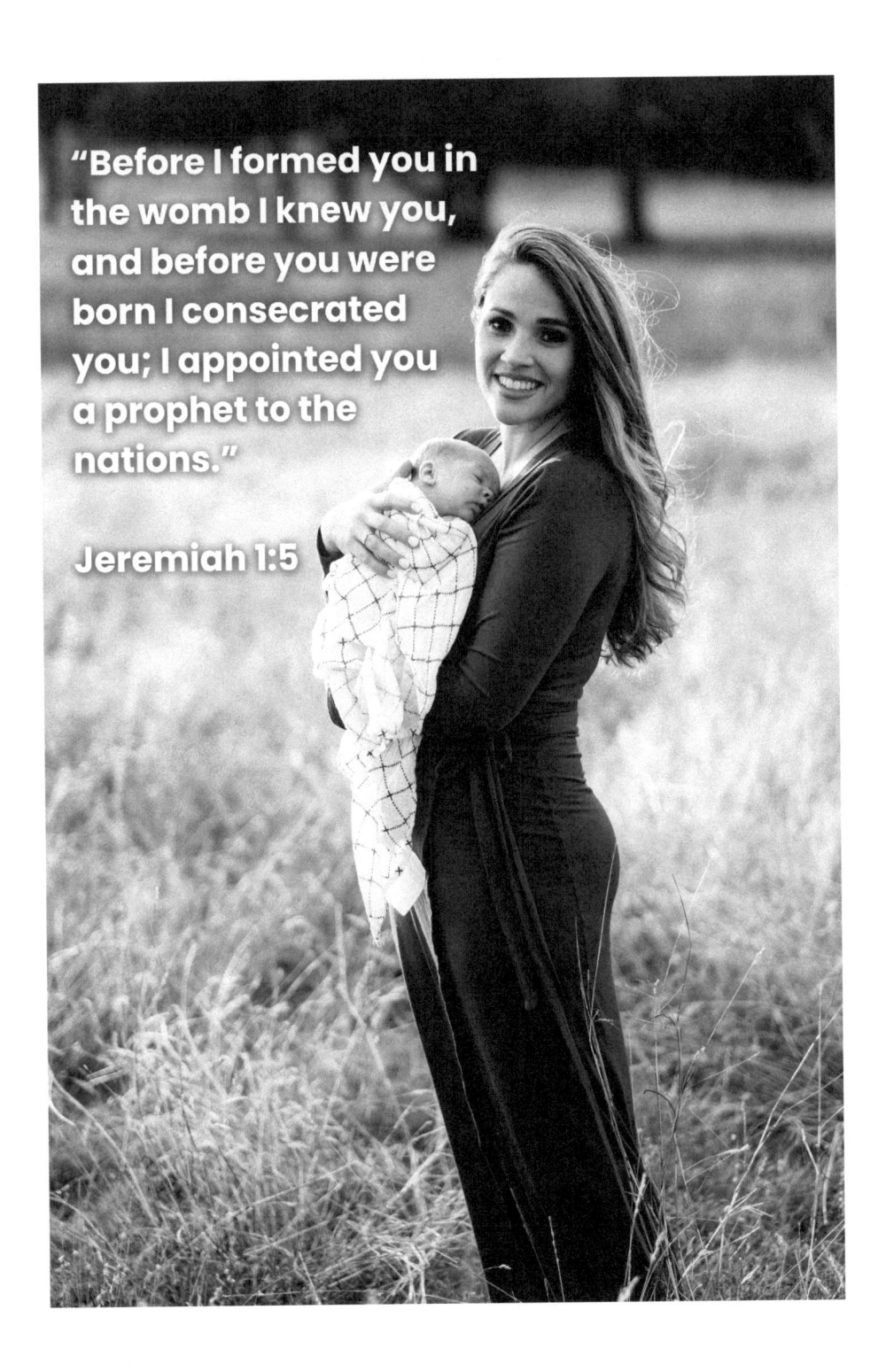

"Before I formed you in the womb I knew you, and before you were born I consecrated you; I appointed you a prophet to the nations."

Jeremiah 1:5

SECRET THREE

Create a Memory to Honor Your Child

Creating a memory to honor your child will look different for everyone.

One of the things my husband and I did to create a special memory was to go out to our son's grave to open the gender results of our second child, as I mentioned in the previous section. While this may be painful for some, we chose to include Jackson in the joy of finding out if he would have a little brother, or a little sister.

Another thing we did was, we saved a little outfit that we had purchased for him, simply as a way to further hold onto memories of him. This brought me joy because I remember the happiness I experienced the day I bought the outfit - I remember the phone conversations with friends in awe that we actually had a child on the way.

So while yes, it is painful to an extent to keep some of these things, I choose to remember the moment of joy, the mental place of happiness that I was in when I purchased them.

I choose to remember the delightment of those moments above the bitter pain.

A wooden letter 'J' sits in his closet, along with his hospital wristband and birth certificate with a hand-signed card from his nurses.

Some dear neighbors and friends brought us fresh roses after his birth, and we kept some of the petals pressed inside of the cards from his funeral.

One of our longtime couple-friends from racing motocross mailed us a gorgeous canvas-printed photo that they'd taken of the sun setting over the ocean near their home in Australia.

I highly suggest doing something that livens your day and brightens your spirit when you think about your child. Yes, while the memories at times are very painful, I choose to focus on the happiness that my son brought to me, as a way for my mind to correlate the joy that he brought to our lives. Although brief, it was fierce and it was real.

"Be strong! Be fearless! Don't be afraid because it is the Lord your God who marches with you. He won't let you down, and he won't abandon you."

Deuteronomy 31:6

Be still and know I am God.

Psalms 46:10

Secret Three
Special Memory Session

Write down special memories and happy thoughts you have about your child.

_____
_____
_____
_____
_____
_____
_____
_____
_____
_____
_____
_____
_____
_____
_____
_____
_____
_____
_____
_____
_____
_____

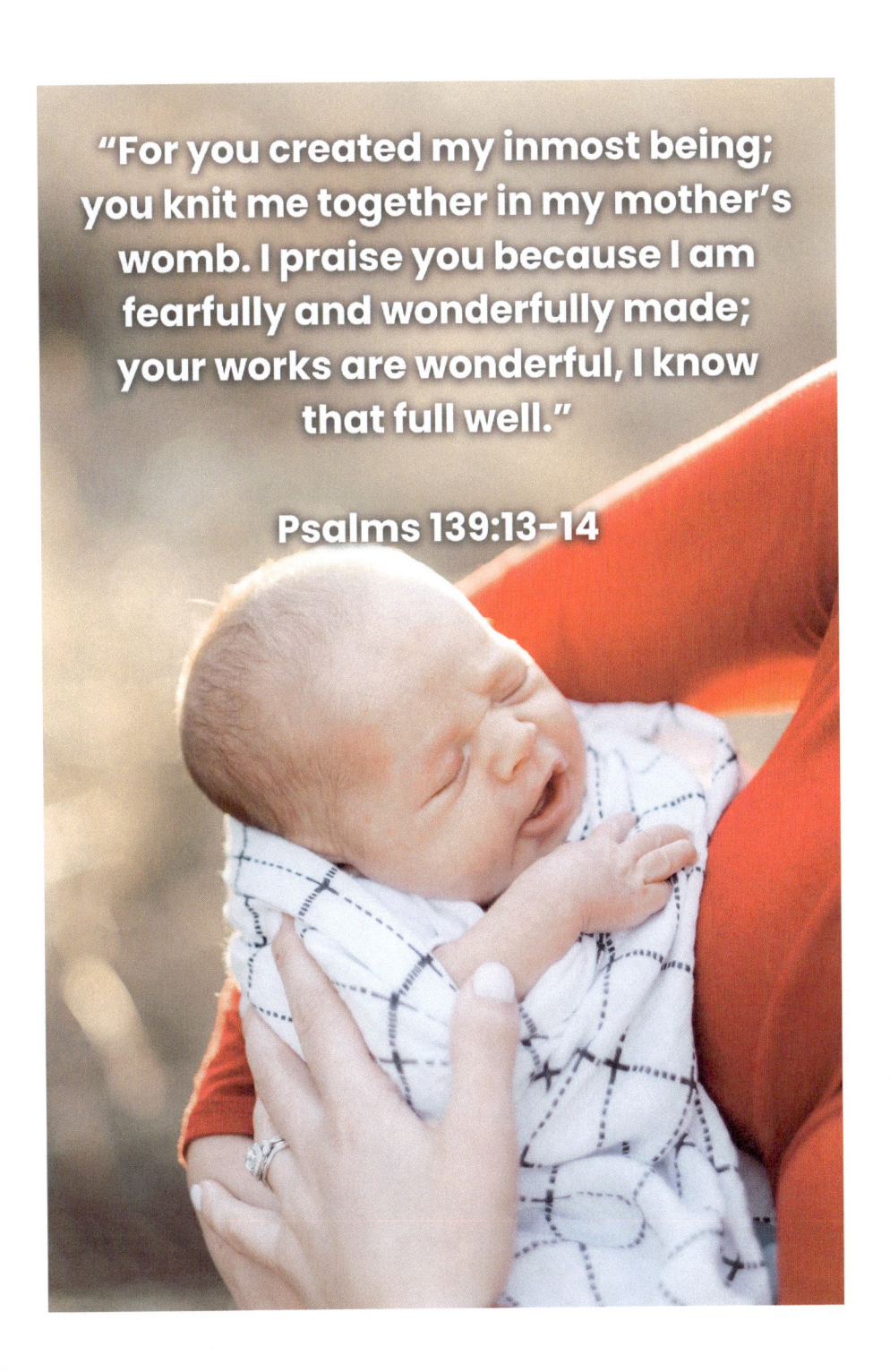

"For you created my inmost being; you knit me together in my mother's womb. I praise you because I am fearfully and wonderfully made; your works are wonderful, I know that full well."

Psalms 139:13-14

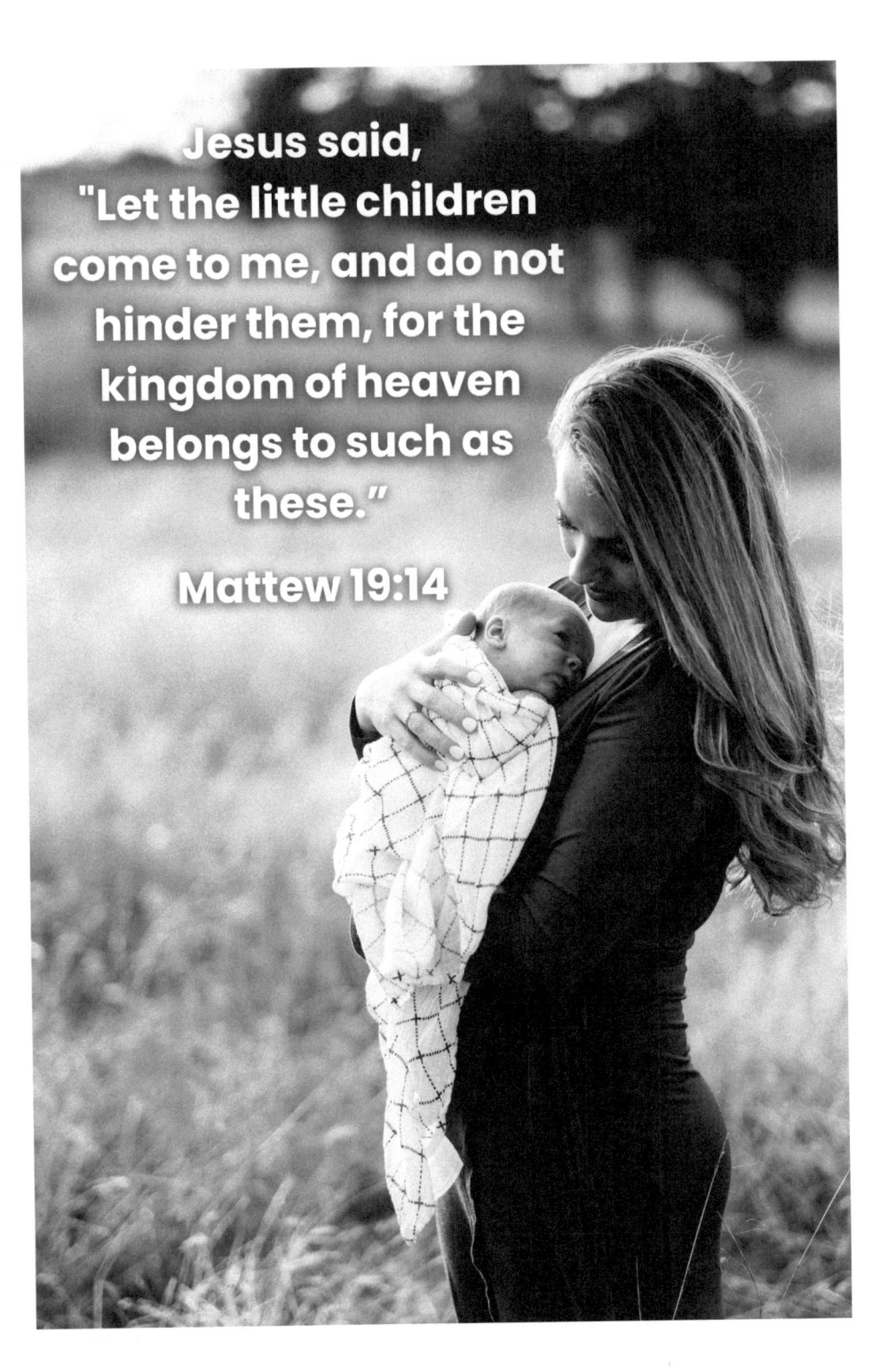

Jesus said, "Let the little children come to me, and do not hinder them, for the kingdom of heaven belongs to such as these."

Mattew 19:14

SECRET FOUR

Talk About Your Child

I learned that it is important to talk about your child for the sake of mentally processing the coming and going of your child.

There is a vast amount of inward healing that must initially take place, and that will progressively continue to take place for the remainder of your life.

This is heavy, yet real. Your child will forever be with you and is a part of who you are now. Your former self has come and gone, and you are learning to adjust and live with the new reality surrounding the vast impact that your precious child had on your life.

Yet, there is a strong key here - only choose to talk about your child with those who are worthy of your story.

What I mean by this is, there are some people who only want to know details of your child's loss and the deep hurt and pain you experienced so that they have new content to talk about with others. Yes, this is a real thing.

Talk About Your Child (continued)

Be very aware of this, and mindful to be purposeful with those whom you choose to share your precious child's story with, less the memory of your child be ridiculed with hurtful words. Your baby was here, your baby is important and your baby changed the world.

Do not give your child's memory and legacy to those who cannot carry the torch and honor your child.

"Children are a gift from the Lord, they are a reward from Him."

-Psalm 127:3

"Blessed are those who mourn, for they shall be comforted."

Matthew 5:4

"The Lord will stand with you and give you strength."

II Timothy 4:17

Secret Four
Special Memory Session

Write down special memories and happy thoughts you have about your child.

_____
_____
_____
_____
_____
_____
_____
_____
_____
_____
_____
_____
_____
_____
_____
_____
_____
_____
_____
_____
_____
_____
_____
_____
_____

"My flesh and my heart may fail, but God is the strength of my heart and my portion forever."

Psalm 73:26

"And so I am sure confident that God, who began this good work in you, will carry it on until it is finished on the Day of Christ Jesus."

Philippians 1:6

SECRET FIVE

Know and Maintain the Sacredness of Your Child

There is a quote which reads, *"Know your worth, you must find the courage to leave the table if respect is no longer being served."* This quote really stick out in my mind thinking about it in relation to my child.

This key goes hand-in-hand with the fourth key, 'Talk About Your Child.'

If you are sharing something special about your child and what you are sharing is not respected or well-received, my recommendation is to not share anything further with someone who does not respect or honor your child's memory.

Oftentimes, those who have never experienced child loss simply do not understand the devastation of it. The reality I learned is, not everyone will 'get it' and understand, and that's okay. They're not your tribe.

Know and Maintain the Sacredness of Your Child (continued)

After the excruciating loss of Jackson, my doctor recommended I take a couple weeks off work. My job at the time was a daily onsite position. When I mentioned that I was requesting to take some time off work, I remember someone saying to me, "You're taking time off work, **why**?" in disbelief as if requesting to take a couple weeks off of work was in some way being dramatic.

I just smiled and never mentioned anything about my son to that person again. I realized, that person had no clue what I'd just gone through. I just kept the legacy of my child sacred and shared very sparingly.

There are also those who simply think it is 'off-putting' to speak of a child who has passed away. Please understand right now that they are simply not worthy of hearing about, or even knowing anything more about your wonderful and precious child.

This may sound harsh, yet I write them off entirely. Meaning, I no longer consider them deserving of knowing anything else about my experience and the child that made me a mother and changed my life.

Know your worth, your child's worth and do everything to protect and keep it sacred.

You've got this, momma.

"May the God of hope fill you with all joy and peace as you trust in Him, so that you may overflow with hope by the power of the Holy Spirit."

Romans 15:13

"Surely goodness and mercy shall follow me all the days of my life, and I shall dwell in the house of the LORD forever."

Psalm 23:6

Secret Five
Special Memory Session

Write down special memories and happy thoughts you have about your child.

_____
_____
_____
_____
_____
_____
_____
_____
_____
_____
_____
_____
_____
_____
_____
_____
_____
_____
_____
_____
_____
_____

His last heartbeat on earth was as quiet as a whisper, yet felt as heavy as a falling tree's shattering thud.

It felt like the earth shook and time was shattered. That was the moment my doctor came into the hospital room and let us know there was nothing more they could do.

My heart pounded in my chest and the heaviest tears filled my eyes as I knew my son would no longer survive.

The minutes became a blur as they seemed to stop, yet I prayed in my heart I would remember every sweet moment that I silently tried to grasp and hold on to.

Beep, beep, beep.

The inevitable was drawing near and my heart would never be the same.

This was our son, and he was perfect.

-EH

I dreamed of knowing him, of holding him longer and seeing his eyes gaze.

While we may never understand why, I know my life is better because of you.

If you're like me, your child is a large reason you continually strive for success. I want to make my son proud. Your child's memory is something that is imprinted within our souls.

It is my strong belief that parents who have lost a child think and act differently than others.

-EH

There would never be enough kisses for him to know my love. He's the one who made me a mother. He is my son.

-EH

As my sons heart beat within me, I listened to the gentle rhythm of our two bodies in sync.

I knew it would be the last time. I knew that any moment that special beating heart would sound no longer.

I knew he was alive and for this moment in time, I felt so much joy.

He was perfect.

-EH

Listed within this book are five simple, yet powerful, strategies that will help you lead your life to a higher level of performance by utilizing the experience you have gained.

Each of the five keys can stand independently of each other, and may be read and practiced in any order you choose. Simply flip to the key that is currently most impactful to you.

-EH

"Trust in the Lord with all your heart and lean not on your own understanding. In all your ways, acknowledge HIm, and He will direct your path."

Proverbs 3:5

In addition, included are various images you may appreciate seeing, especially those from behind-the-scenes of my life with my children.

Some insight to living a more purposeful life in the midst of your pain may be new, while other keys may be more familiar and therefore easier to implement. I hope you find them all comforting, and that you carry them close to your heart.

-EH

I carried you for every second of your life, and I will love you for every second of mine.

-EH

At times you will feel comforted, and other times you will feel that you are just broken. Either way, you are justified to feel the way you do. One thing is for certain, you as a parent think and act differently now.

In the midst of sorrow, my child will always make my joy complete. I am grateful for him and the time, although brief, will forever be cherished.

-EH

I will always look upon you with awe and wonder, as you have filled my heart with many joyous things.

-Ell

One Last Message!

My experience losing Jackson gave me personally a different perspective on life and death. While extremely difficult to grasp, my basis of faith in Christ has been the solid ground to keep things in perspective for me. I believe there is a heaven where Jackson is today with Jesus. If someone does not believe that, I can certainly understand that the grief of losing a child would more than likely be too much for some to bear. Their child's death would leave them in a place in life that would be extremely difficult to accept and overcome.

I encourage you to not dwell on the tragedy, yet live in a place of peace and healing. This life does not always make sense, and we cannot always define the things that we wish would have happened instead. Some things truly are out of our control, yet there is a place of hope in Jesus Christ. Please trust this. If you have any questions, please reach out. My loss has actually helped me understand life, and today I am living even more fulfilled because I strive everyday to make my son so proud of me! That is the basis of my joy and hope.

While loss can lead to unrelenting pain, I believe there is always a silver-lining to everything that happens to us in life. I would never have chosen for Jackson to pass away, yet I know that having him in my life has made me a better mother and a better person for having gone through it. I encourage you to cherish the moments and be grateful for the time you had with your child.

-Emily Harris

October 27, 2019

This is my second son, Cason. We went out to Jackson's grave on the anniversary of his due date to spread flowers and spend time with him.

XOXO

October 19, 2018

This is Cason right before we went home from the hospital after he was born.

"I am proof that God answers prayers."

Since losing her firstborn son, Jackson, Emily has gone on to maintain two successful pregnancies which she carried until exactly 37 weeks and 4 days with both her son Cason (second pregnancy), and her daughter Claire (third pregnancy).

A surgical cerclage was placed at 22 weeks, after being diagnosed with cervical incompetency, in order to support her pregnancies, allowing her to reach a longer gestational session. She was induced for her deliveries in order to maintain a safe environment for her babies. A Level IV (the highest level) Neonatal Intensive Care Unit (NICU) is in place at Medical City Dallas where Emily delivered all of her children.

*Special **FREE** Bonus Gift for You*
To help you achieve more balance and stability surrounding infant loss, there are
FREE BONUS RESOURCES for you at:
www.FreeGiftFromEmily.com
In-depth training and insight on how can proactively process deep emotions, stop blaming yourself and achieve peace to create a more meaningful life after infant loss.

ABOUT EMILY

Emily Harris is recognized as one of the most requested, in-demand business and motivational keynote speakers and marketing consultants in the United States. She has been featured in multiple magazines, has spoken at colleges and has been approached by many to learn and glean insight from her experience regarding the inspirational approaches that make her such a stand-out leader in her field - not just regarding infant loss, but in life. Emily has spoken to multiple CEOs and leaders of large corporations, associations, business groups, colleges and youth organizations. Emily can speak for groups ranging from 20-20,000. Emily is the behind-the-scenes, go-to marketing advisor for many top speakers, authors, business professionals, entrepreneurs, CEOs and thought leaders. With more than 15 years in the business marketing field, her knowledge and expertise are second-to-none and she is an absolute joy to work with.

Additional Resources

Emily has also created a step-by-step **'Mindset for Mom'** course specifically created for women who have experienced infant loss. One of the main topics of discussion is about how infant loss can also affect a relationship with a partner or spouse. Through her own experience, she has created scenarios and strategies to overcome one of the most trying situations that can come between two people in a relationship. To find her course, please visit **www.FreeGiftFromEmily.com** and join the **When Feathers Fall** Facebook community group.

Scan the QR code for FREE resources and join the private community of mothers experiencing a similar situation:

https://www.facebook.com/groups/900950630756603

Special *FREE* Bonus Gift for You

To help you achieve more balance and stability surrounding infant loss, there are

FREE BONUS RESOURCES
for you at:
www.FreeGiftFromEmily.com

- **In-depth training and insight on how can proactively process deep emotions, stop blaming yourself and achieve peace to create a more meaningful life after infant loss.**

Acknowledgements

Through the years, many have shared ideas, mentoring and support that has impacted my life, each in a different way. It's impossible to thank everyone and I apologize for anyone not listed. Please know, that I appreciate you greatly.

Thank you to my husband, Jeremy Harris. I never knew the journey we'd be on when we said 'I do.'

Photo captured at El Morro Spanish Fortress in San Juan, Puerto Rico the day before Jeremy and Emily Harris wed.

April 19, 2014

WHEN FEATHERS FALL™

Made in the USA
Columbia, SC
04 October 2024